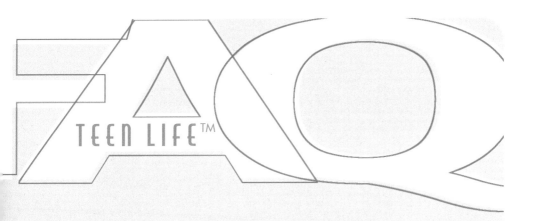

TEEN LIFE™

FREQUENTLY ASKED QUESTIONS ABOUT

Shoplifting and Theft

ROSEN
PUBLISHING®

New York

Published in 2012 by The Rosen Publishing Group, Inc.
29 East 21st Street, New York, NY 10010

Library of Congress Cataloging-in-Publication Data

Sonneborn, Liz.
Frequently asked questions about shoplifting and theft/Liz
Sonneborn.—1st ed.
    p. cm.—(FAQ, teen life)
Includes bibliographical references and index.
ISBN 978-1-4488-5558-2 (library binding)
1. Shoplifting—Juvenile literature. 2. Shoplifting—Prevention—
Juvenile literature. I. Title.
HV6652.S66 2012
364.16'2—dc22

                                                    2011015173

Manufactured in China

CPSIA Compliance Information: Batch #W12YA. For further information, contact Rosen Publishing, New York, New York,
at 1-800-237-9932.

HOW COMMON IS SHOPLIFTING?

On December 12, 2001, the surveillance cameras in a Saks Fifth Avenue store in Beverly Hills, California, recorded the image of a dark-haired, petite woman as she walked through the store. While she walked among the display tables, the two shopping bags and the garment bag she was lugging seemed to get bigger and bigger.

The woman bought a few items and walked out of the store, where security guards confronted her. They accused her of shoplifting, escorted her back to the store's holding room, and waited for the police to arrive. The guards found in her bags $5,560 worth of unpaid merchandise, including a sweater worth $750 and a pair of socks that retailed for $80. The woman denied their charges, insisting that she thought her assistant had paid for the items. The police were not convinced.

The Ryder Case

This series of events is hardly unheard of. After all, every day in stores across the United States, security personnel nab customers for shoplifting, or taking goods without paying for them. Many, if not most, claim innocence, citing equally implausible excuses.

But the woman in the Beverly Hills Saks wasn't just any shoplifter. She was Winona Ryder, the thirty-year-old movie star who had been a famous actress since her teen years. At the time, Ryder was commanding a salary of up to $6 million per film. The press and the tabloids went crazy after learning about her arrest. They all asked the same question—why on earth was a talented, beautiful, intelligent young film star shoplifting? Why would such a privileged person, with plenty of money to buy whatever she wanted, stoop to stealing from a retail store that she had to know was full of cameras?

In the glare of the media spotlight, Ryder went to trial. The jury found her guilty of grand theft and vandalism. Although she faced three years and eight months in prison, the judge instead sentenced Ryder to three years' probation and 480 hours of community service, and ordered her to pay about $10,000 in fines and restitution. Following the trial, Ryder avoided the public eye. After about five years, she again began to seek out small film roles, hoping to become known as something other than the world's most famous shoplifter. In 2007, she gave an interview to *Vogue* magazine, in which she discussed her arrest. Ryder finally admitted that she was guilty, although she tried to

In 2002, the trial of actress Winona Ryder made news around the world. Ryder was accused of shoplifting more than $5,000 worth of merchandise from a store in Beverly Hills, California.

explain away her actions. She blamed her shoplifting on "confusion" brought on by a dependence on prescription painkillers.

Profile of a Shoplifter

The over-the-top news coverage of Ryder's legal mess brought the crime of shoplifting to the public's attention. For anyone working in retail, though, shoplifting certainly isn't anything new. The term "shoplifting" came into use more than one hundred years ago, when the first department stores sprang up in major cities. Store employees noticed that some of their customers, even wealthy ladies, were occasionally helping themselves to merchandise. Not wanting to accuse their high-society customers of stealing, stores came up with the less ugly-sounding word "shoplifting" to describe what these customers were doing.

As more retail stores were built across the United States, shoplifting became more common. According to the 2009 television documentary *The Truth About Shoplifting*, about 80 percent of Americans have shoplifted at least once in their lives. Interviewed in the film, shoplifting expert Terrence Shulman estimated that about 10 percent do so on a regular basis.

Justifying Stealing

Deep down, nearly all shoplifters know that what they are doing is wrong. The exceptions are very small children, who don't have the ability to understand the concept of private property. Older kids generally have been taught not to steal. But overwhelmed by the sight of toys or candy in a store, they often

Professional thieves are often very skilled at their job. His face hidden by a hood, this bicycle thief came prepared with a heavy-duty wire cutter to destroy a bike lock.

simply can't control the impulse to grab whatever they want most. Children with older brothers or sisters are especially likely to shoplift things their siblings have but their parents feel are too grown-up for them. Some kids steal items so that they can give presents to other children, hoping to win their friendship with the shoplifted trinkets. Still, most children who shoplift stop when they are older and have a more developed sense of right and wrong.

Certainly, nearly all teens know it is wrong to shoplift. But they are especially vulnerable to its allure. Peer pressure often plays a role in the decision to steal. Teens' friends might try to humiliate reluctant shoplifters, making them feel like goody-two-shoes if they don't join in. Teenagers also feel enormous pressure to fit in with their circle of friends. All too often, they feel like outsiders if they don't own the right kinds of clothes or cell phone or whatever new thing is popular with their peers. So they are willing to resort to stealing to get these items. According to a survey by the Josephson Institute of Ethics of forty-three thousand high school students, about one in three boys and one in four girls admitted they had shoplifted within the last twelve months in 2010. In addition, 21 percent said they had stolen from a parent or another relative, and 18 percent admitted they had taken something from a friend.

Teen shoplifters are often good at finding ways of justifying what they are doing. They have friends who have gotten away with it, so they convince themselves that shoplifting is no big deal. Because shoplifting is a subject that parents and teachers rarely talk about, many teens also see shoplifting as a fairly minor offense. The more time passes, the easier it becomes to justify their stealing. As one teen girl explained in "Shoplifting—Girls Who Steal," an article in *Seventeen* magazine, "At first, you think a lot about what you're doing and the fact that it's wrong. But after a while, it becomes less and less real somehow. It becomes such a game, you don't worry anymore if it's right or wrong."

A Victimless Crime?

When confessing to shoplifting in *Vogue*, Winona Ryder offered another justification used by teens and adults alike. "I didn't have this tremendous sense of guilt because I hadn't hurt anyone," she said. "Had I physically harmed someone or caused harm to a human being, I think it would have been an entirely different experience."

Many people similarly assume that shoplifting is a victimless crime. But in reality, everyone everywhere pays for shoplifting. To make up for the profits that stores lose to stealing, they have to raise prices on all the goods they sell. According to *The Truth About Shoplifting*, the average person pays about $440 a year more on products than he or she would have if no one ever shoplifted.

Many stores place their security cameras where shoppers can't help but see them. They hope the cameras will dissuade any would-be shoplifters from stealing.

As shoplifting becomes more prevalent, stores feel they have to do something to stop it. This need has created the loss prevention industry. Stores now have to hire security guards to help them curb shoplifting. Many also purchase expensive surveillance cameras and other security equipment. Of course, all of these added costs are passed on to customers in the form of higher prices.

Stores, especially small ones preyed upon by professional thieves, sometimes find themselves losing so much money that they have to go out of business. In that case, shoplifters are responsible for putting everyone who worked in those stores out of a job. In addition, when shoplifters steal goods, they are cheating local and state governments out of sales tax. These governments then see a substantial reduction in the revenue they need for schools, roads, and services that benefit all of their citizens.

Shoplifters, too, often pay a high personal price for shoplifting. If they get caught, they might have to go to court or even jail. They will also likely lose the trust of their friends and family once the news of their arrest is out. Even shoplifters who never get caught usually suffer severe consequences for their actions. No one else might know what they are doing, but their conscience won't let them forget. Feelings of guilt begin to gnaw at them, always challenging their sense of themselves as decent and moral people. In the end, for many shoplifters, the worst punishment for their crime is the loss of their own self-respect.

WHY DO PEOPLE SHOPLIFT?

The reason why some people shoplift is obvious: they want something without paying for it. In the case of poverty-stricken people, that something is often a necessity, such as food or clothing. When the poor shoplift, it is usually not because they don't want to pay for the goods they take, but because they don't have the money to pay. Their circumstances force them to make a difficult decision. Consider the case of an impoverished mother who does not have the money she needs to buy food for her family. She might find herself in the almost impossible situation of having to choose between letting her children go hungry and committing a crime that could land her in jail. But poor people, desperate and driven by need, are a small minority of shoplifters. Most shoplifters have other, more complicated motivations for their actions.

Most shoplifters do not plan on stealing when they enter a store. Usually, they act on impulse, grabbing an item and stuffing it in a bag or a pocket when they think no one is looking.

Professional Shoplifters

The least sympathetic of all shoplifters are the professionals. Professional shoplifters, often called boosters, are likely career criminals. They would probably commit other crimes such as burglary or robbery if they didn't see shoplifting as an attractive alternative. Many find shoplifting an easier crime to commit, with less risk of getting hurt or getting arrested. Some professional shoplifters work alone. Others are members of the hundreds of shoplifting gangs in operation in the United States at any given time. A substantial number are probably affiliated with organized crime.

For skilled professionals, shoplifting is a low-risk, high-profit crime. They target items such as over-the-counter drugs that are small and expensive. Many hide their loot in foil-lined bags called booster bags. These bags prevent sensor tags on the stolen items from setting off an alarm when they leave the store.

Boosters sell shoplifted items to fences, criminals who traffic in stolen goods. Fences often seek out drug addicts and people with gambling addictions to work for them. They know these people are continually desperate for money but are not usually violent, hardened criminals, which most fences, for their own safety, want to avoid dealing with. Frequently, fences provide boosters with "shopping" lists of items they are interested in with the prices they are willing to pay for them. Generally, fences offer boosters just a small percentage of the retail value of their stolen goods, but they pay fast. For drug addicts desperate for a fix, fences may even advance them money because they know they will be repaid after the addicts' next shoplifting spree.

These low-level fences, or street fences, then sell the stolen goods to higher-level fences. These criminals, in turn, resell the shoplifted items to discount stores, on the Internet, or at flea markets. There, they are sold to the public at deep discounts from their retail prices. If you find a Web site or a discount store that is selling small-size mer-chandise at incredible prices, think twice about buying anything. Most likely, the items on sale were shoplifted.

Employee Theft

The vast majority of shoplifters are amateurs. They don't steal things for a living. They instead shoplift items for themselves or their friends. Many of these people know the stores they steal from well. In fact, they work in them.

The Truth About Shoplifting reported that stores in North America lose about $40 billion a year in what they call "shrink." Shrink is the money lost by retailers through stealing and administra-tive errors. Employee theft accounts for about half of that.

For some employees, the temptation of being around displays of consumer goods all day just proves too much to resist. For others, stealing is a way of getting back at their employers. Especially at big chain stores, employees often come and go

Shops that sell small, but expensive goods—such as this Apple computer store—are particularly vulnerable to shoplifting. To protect themselves, they often invest a good deal of money in security personnel and surveillance systems.

quickly, without much training. They feel little loyalty toward their employers, which can make people feel that it's OK to help themselves to a gift card or a pair of earrings every now and then. Workers at many retail stores are also paid low wages. Believing that they are not paid adequately for the work they do, shoplifting employees can convince themselves that, instead of committing theft, they are just taking what the company already owes them.

Of course, their employers are likely to see things differently. Employees who get caught stealing are sure to be fired. But because some stores have policies requiring them to prosecute all shoplifters, thieving employees might also find themselves arrested, even if all they took was a candy bar.

The Lure of Luxuries

Other amateur shoplifters are customers. They steal for a wide variety of reasons. Some shoplifters do it because they want things they can't afford. This is often true of teenage shoplifters. They usually have a limited amount of spending money, while at the same time they want to earn their friends' admiration by showing off expensive possessions. For this reason, the first items that many teen girls steal are cosmetics and perfumes—commonly costly items that are easy to tuck into a purse or a pocket.

Sometimes, these shoplifters feel little remorse because they are convinced that they deserve these little luxuries. Without a hint of conscience, one teenaged shoplifter quoted in "The Beauty Snatchers," an article in *Real Beauty* magazine, justified her behavior with the statement, "I can wear better brand-name beauty products that I might not otherwise be able to afford. And that gives me more self-confidence."

But for others, the joys of having luxury items that they couldn't otherwise afford dull quickly as their conscience gets the better of them. Teens, especially, might feel a buzz after they steal something with their friends egging them on. But when they are alone, they are suddenly overwhelmed by a strong sense of guilt. Often, the guilt is so powerful that they vow never to shoplift again.

For the Thrill

It isn't surprising when shoplifters steal merchandise they want. But many times, what they pocket is almost irrelevant to them. The main motivation of these shoplifters is not to get new things. Instead, they are seeking the experience, particularly the way that shoplifting makes them feel. These shoplifters will steal anything, even pilfering items that are completely useless to them. For instance, shoplifting expert Terrence Shulman told *USA Today* that one person he treated for habitual shoplifting had stolen a set of drill bits, even though the person did not even own a drill.

One popular reason that people cite for shoplifting is the thrill of it. Natural thrill-seekers, young people are especially prone to seek excitement by shoplifting. When they are bored,

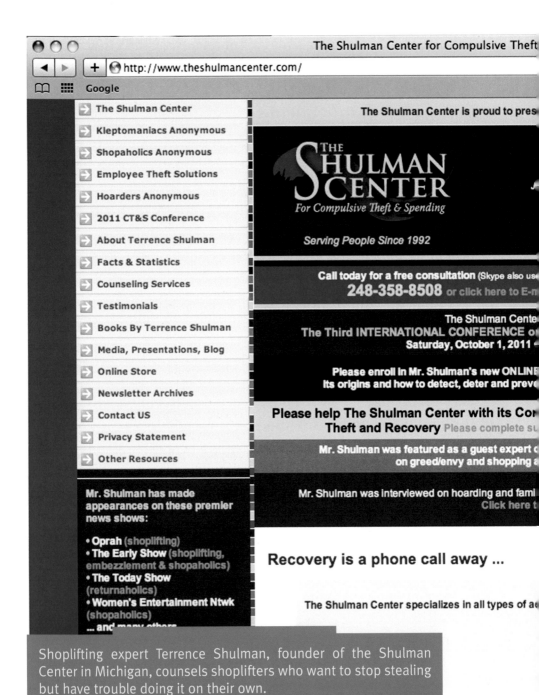

Shoplifting expert Terrence Shulman, founder of the Shulman Center in Michigan, counsels shoplifters who want to stop stealing but have trouble doing it on their own.

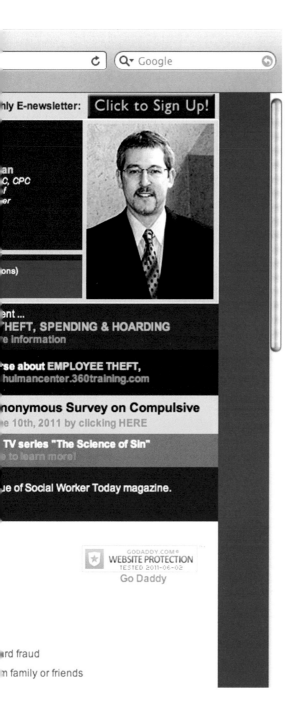

either alone or in groups, they enjoy getting themselves into dangerous situations. In an article titled "The Thrill of Theft," which appeared in *Newsweek* magazine, one high school student explained the rush she got from shoplifting: "Your heart starts to race, and all you can think about is getting out of the store. It's like, 'I've taken what I need to take, let's get out of here.' But I get really excited because I'm thinking 'I already got a bunch of stuff in my bag, and I can get a whole lot more.'"

Young people are also driven to shoplift because it gives them a sense of freedom, independence, and control. Teens can become frustrated by all the rules they are expected to follow—both those set down by their teachers at school and by their parents at home. High-achieving students might feel particularly weighed down by the expectations placed on them. For these teens, shoplifting is a way of acting out. They see it as a quiet little rebellion that, as long as they don't get caught, won't do anything to tarnish their reputation among the adults they work so hard to please.

Shoplifting might also satisfy an urge for revenge. When people feel they have been wronged, they tend to want to strike out in anger. Teenagers, for instance, might be mad at their parents. But because young people are so dependent on their parents, they are often reluctant to confront them directly. Instead, they take out their anger by shoplifting. Often, these shoplifters tell themselves that the store they are stealing from deserves it for charging prices that are too high. In some cases, of course, revenge shoplifters do have real grievances with a store. Customers, for instance, might decide to shoplift if they feel that a store's staff has been rude or disrespectful toward them.

Filling an Emotional Void

People who feel that they are unloved or underappreciated sometimes turn to shoplifting. They are often in unhappy relationships with friends and family. Frequently, they are caregivers to ailing relatives. These people are often extremely generous with their time and attention, helping others get through difficult times, but secretly they resent that no one seems to be there for them. Shoplifting, then,

Boredom, anxiety, and anger drive some teenagers to shoplift. Often, they don't care what they steal. They just want the rush of excitement that shoplifting gives them.

becomes a way of rewarding themselves for their sacrifices. The stolen object is something of a thank-you gift that they give to themselves. This common psychological equation of shoplifting with gift giving probably explains why some shoplifters steal more around their birthdays and during the Christmas season.

A sense of personal loss can also inspire shoplifting. For example, as cited in the *Allure* magazine article "Crimes of Fashion," one study by shoplifting expert Will Cupchik found that nearly 30 percent of shoplifters had recently known someone diagnosed with cancer. His findings suggest that shoplifting can help fill a void in people who are suffering deeply, often in silence. At least for a moment, shoplifting allows them to escape overwhelming emotional pain.

In much the same way, others use shoplifting to relieve anxiety. When people feel they are in situations that are beyond their control, they might shoplift to give themselves a sense that they can take action and exert power within their world. For these people, shoplifting can be a very effective, if ultimately self-destructive, way of relieving stress.

Faced with many day-to-day pressures, teenagers are especially susceptible to turning to shoplifting during stressful times. "I Caught My Son Stealing," an article published in *Good Housekeeping* magazine, profiled one such teenager identified as Bobby. Bobby began shoplifting after his family moved to a new house and he started attending a school where he didn't know anyone. Feeling alone and lost, Bobby started stealing from his family and from other students to relieve his stress. He soon graduated to shoplifting from a record store and lying to his parents about where he got the stolen items. After it came out what Bobby was doing, a guidance counselor determined that, on a subconscious level, Bobby's stealing wasn't just a way of making himself feel better. It was also a way of getting his neglectful parents' attention. According to the counselor, "In Bobby's case, all the changes in his life must have fueled his insecurity. I think his stealing was a cry for help. I think he wanted to get caught."

Myths and Facts

All teenagers shoplift and steal.

Fact: ●▶ Teenagers shoplift for many different reasons—to get things they want, to impress their friends, to get their parents' attention, and more. But most teenagers never shoplift or steal anything. They resist whatever personal or peer pressure they experience to take things that don't belong to them. Many honest teens, though, suffer from the stigma that all teenagers are potential shoplifters. If you have ever walked through a store with a clerk watching you like a hawk, you know just how annoying that stereotype can be.

Shoplifters only steal things they want or need.

Fact: ●▶ Poor people sometimes shoplift food to feed themselves and their families. Other people, with some income but not enough to buy luxury goods, steal to get merchandise they want but can't afford. But many shoplifters steal things they don't want and sometimes can't even use. For these people, shoplifting is less about getting stuff than it is about filling some emotional need. They may be depressed, anxious, or angry. Shoplifting gives them a high that, for a short period of time, relieves the emotional strain of these negative emotions.

Stores can afford any lost profits due to shoplifting.

Fact: Because of shoplifting, American stores lose billions of dollars every year. That doesn't include any of the money they spend to prevent shoplifting or prosecute thieves. With the costs of shoplifting being so high, no store can afford to ignore it. To make a profit, stores have to raise prices to make up for the lost income. If you get mad at a store for its high prices, you might be tempted to shoplift there. But remember, those prices that make you so angry are probably as high as they are because of the shoplifters who came before you. If you shoplift, you are just adding to the problem.

three

IS SHOPLIFTING ADDICTIVE?

In the 1890s, psychiatrists diagnosed a new mental disorder. They called it kleptomania. It is defined as an irresistible urge to steal things, especially things that the thief does not need or necessarily want. When kleptomaniacs shoplift, they almost always do it without forethought. In fact, they may not even be aware of what they are doing at all. People often label all shoplifters as "kleptos," but very few people receive a formal psychiatric diagnosis of kleptomania.

Many experts, however, believe that there are far more compulsive shoplifters than the psychiatric community acknowledges. Compulsive shoplifters, once they develop the need to steal, find it very hard, if not impossible, to shut off that impulse. In this sense, many mental health experts believe that, for some people, shoplifting can become addictive.

Tension and Relief

For compulsive shoplifters, stealing from stores involves a pre-dictable wave of emotions. Imagine a teenage girl named Abby is shopping in a drugstore. She is walking through the cosmetic aisle, lost in thought about the American history report she needs to finish. Out of the corner of her eye, she suddenly spots a lipstick. She almost never wears makeup, but that's not important. All that matters is the incredible tension she feels after seeing the lipstick, a powerful feeling that compels her to act.

Abby impulsively slips the lipstick into her coat pocket. Knowing it's there only adds to her anxiety. She then notices a salesperson nearby. "Did he see what I did?" she asks herself. Then Abby looks up. There is a surveillance camera on the wall. "Did it record me shoving the lipstick in my coat?" By this point, the tension Abby feels is almost overwhelming.

In this heightened state, Abby decides to head for the door, all the while sure that she will be nabbed by store security at any moment. She opens the door and walks through, and nobody follows her. She keeps walking across the parking lot, and still nothing. Then it comes, the release of her tension and the incredible high of relief.

Soon, though, remorse sets in. "Why did I do that?" Abby wonders later at home, when she's hiding the lipstick she will never use in the back of a drawer. "I know shoplifting is wrong. What if I got caught? If I got arrested, my parents would be humiliated. And everyone at school would find out, too." The

Teen girl shoplifters often start by stealing nail polish, lipstick, and other cosmetics. They can impress their friends with these luxury goods, which, because of their small size, are particularly easy to pocket.

more she thinks about what could have happened, the more upset and depressed she feels. It's only a matter of time before she again seeks relief the only way she knows how—through the exhilaration that comes from stealing.

Getting Hooked

The emotions that Abby feels are common among shoplifters. Even children might experience the same cycle of tension, relief, and remorse. But most people, after one or two shoplifting adventures, will rationally see that the risks involved outweigh the benefits. Many others who are regular shoplifters during their teen years might stop stealing when they get older. They naturally "age out" of shoplifting because they no longer need the thrill that it gave them.

But some people cannot stop themselves from continuing to chase the high they get from shoplifting. No matter how bad they feel later, their remorse gets cancelled out by the memory of the glorious sense of relief they felt. Their urge to steal grows stronger, as does the need to shoplift more expensive items in ever-riskier situations in order to keep the rush coming. They often start stealing from their friends and family, despite knowing that their actions might forever poison their closest relationships.

Some shoplifters who fall into these patterns might suffer from an imbalance of the chemical serotonin. Serotonin imbalance in the nervous system appears to cause similar obsessive behaviors, such as compulsive gambling and constant hand washing.

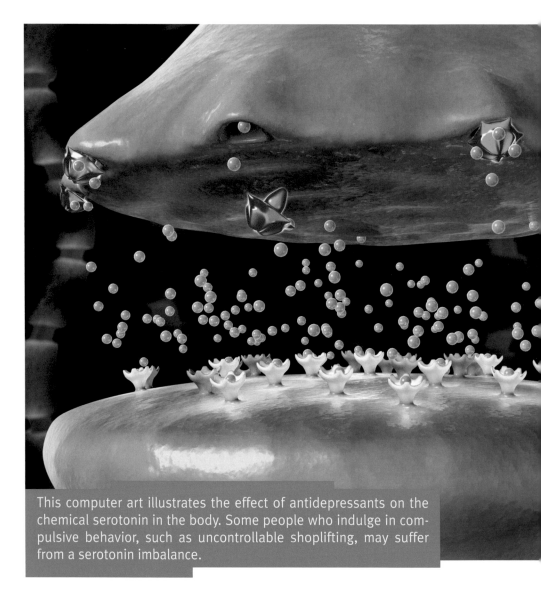

This computer art illustrates the effect of antidepressants on the chemical serotonin in the body. Some people who indulge in compulsive behavior, such as uncontrollable shoplifting, may suffer from a serotonin imbalance.

People are also often driven to shoplift by underlying psychological problems. For instance, they may be chronically anxious, angry, or depressed. If these conditions go undiagnosed and untreated, sufferers desperately seek out any kind of relief they

can get, however temporary. Some turn to drugs and alcohol. But others get hooked on the high provided by shoplifting. For them, stealing offers a welcome relief from their emotional problems. Unfortunately, it also often prevents them from facing their real psychological issues and seeking treatment for them.

Multiple Compulsions

It is also not unusual for compulsive shoplifters to have other, equally destructive coping techniques. Many, for instance, have problems with alcohol and drugs. In addition, they might indulge in other compulsive behaviors. They might go on wild shopping sprees, indulge in uncontrollable eating binges, or get caught up in gambling.

Shoplifting is particularly common in young women who have eating disorders, such as anorexia and bulimia. (People with anorexia have an intense fear of gaining weight, so they eat very little food. People with bulimia overeat and then throw up.) In an article titled "The Lure of Shoplifting" in *Good Housekeeping*, one teen shoplifter explained the link between her attempts at controlling her weight and her shoplifting: "Weight has always been an issue with me. I would shoplift when I was trying to diet; I couldn't have food, so I would try to fill myself up in another way. It was my reward for keeping myself thin."

Tennis star Jennifer Capriati was arrested for stealing a $15 ring from a mall store in 1993. Like a substantial number of other young shoplifters, Capriati suffered from an eating disorder, bulimia, in addition to compulsive shoplifting.

The most famous bulimic shoplifter is tennis champion Jennifer Capriati. In 1993, when she was seventeen, she was arrested after she stole a $15 ring at a mall. Capriati has blamed the anxiety caused by her sudden fame as the reason for her shoplifting and bulimia. In "Crimes of Fashion," an article in *Allure*, she was quoted as saying, "When I looked in a mirror, all I saw was this distorted image. I was so ugly and fat, and I more or less wanted to kill myself." The self-hatred that Capriati described is common in people with both eating disorders and problems with shoplifting.

There is, however, one big difference between shoplifting and other similar compulsive behaviors. When compulsive gamblers lose all of their money, others notice. When compulsive shoppers max out their credit cards, others notice. When compulsive eaters gain a dangerous amount of weight, others notice. But if they don't get caught, compulsive shoplifters can hide their obsessive behavior from the world. Sometimes, people suffer the guilt and shame of shoplifting for decades without even their closest friends and family members knowing there is anything wrong.

system they have in place. By making their security efforts so visible, they hope that shoplifters will think twice before committing theft. However, obvious security systems can also annoy honest customers, who feel they are being treated like potential criminals for no good reason. Some stores, therefore, prefer to hide their security measures. They might place cameras in clocks and smoke alarms, and dress their security guards in the clothes of average shoppers instead of in uniforms.

Big stores, especially those that are part of large chains, are investing in increasingly sophisticated technology to help them collar thieves. To monitor every corner of their stores, they use digital closed-circuit television, which delivers very sharp images. Some combine cameras with computer programs that can detect movements that people commonly make when shoplifting. An even more sophisticated security measure is the placement of computer chips in merchandise. Through a Global Positioning System (GPS), stores can use these chips to track the location of stolen goods. This security technique is largely used to find gangs of professional thieves or their fences.

Chains also often hire their own teams of detectives. Police departments, already stretched to the limit investigating violent crimes, do not generally have the resources to hunt down shoplifting rings. Store detectives, therefore, work to compile evidence that they can then turn over to the police. Often, detectives from competing stores share information because they all benefit by putting shoplifting gangs out of business.

Deciding to Prosecute

Some stores have policies that require them to prosecute all shoplifters. Saks Fifth Avenue, for instance, had Winona Ryder arrested in 2001 because of its no-tolerance policy, despite the fact that the incident drew the company into an unwelcome media firestorm. Such policies discourage shoplifting because thieves know they are in for serious trouble if they get caught. It is also a deterrent for professional thieves. To avoid no-tolerance polices, professionals are likely to target other stores where they think the risk of arrest is not so great.

However, other stores are not inclined to call the authorities when they detect a shoplifter. When stores don't come down hard on thieves, they know they might earn a reputation as easy marks. Yet the cost and hassle of prosecuting offenders seem too great to some businesses, particularly small stores with limited resources. As a co-owner of a boutique in Los Angeles, California, explained to *Allure* in 2002, "[H]onestly, if you catch them, it's generally not worth it to call the cops." Taking legal action, she added, required "such a stream of paperwork" that it was a waste of her time.

Some large chains have also made a practical decision not to prosecute everyone who steals from their stores. For instance, Wal-Mart, the largest retailer in the United States, loosened its policy in 2006. It announced that it would no longer prosecute first-time shoplifters who steal less than $25 or are over sixty-five years of age. Wal-Mart decided to focus the energies of its security personnel on catching thieves involved in professional shoplifting rings instead of making an example of the average first-time shoplifter.

There are still other reasons why stores are reluctant to push for prosecution. Some fear lawsuits. If a store accuses an innocent person of shoplifting, it can open itself up to a charge of false arrest. Others are so afraid of getting a reputation for racial profiling—that is, targeting racial minorities with charges of shoplifting—that they might shy away from punishing shoplifters in any way that could become part of the public record. Prosecuting a shoplifter also means that the police will hold the stolen merchandise as evidence while the case makes its way through the legal system. If the merchandise is expensive, a store might decide it's more important to get the stolen goods back on its shelves than it is to punish the thief.

Getting Nabbed

Not all stores have formal shoplifting policies, and if they do, they are often not made public. So when shoplifters get caught, they usually have no idea what's going to happen to them. Generally, security guards wait for suspected shoplifters to leave the store before confronting them. (If they are nabbed in the store, suspects can always claim that they were intending to pay but they just hadn't finished shopping yet.) When guards discover shoplifters with merchandise hidden under their coats or in their bags, they expect to hear, "Oh, I forgot

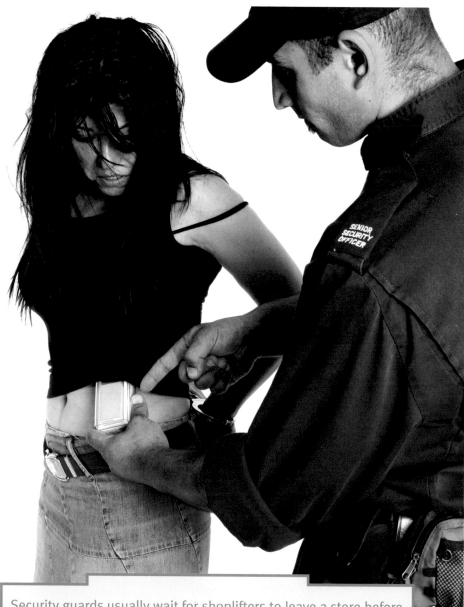

Security guards usually wait for shoplifters to leave a store before confronting them. Otherwise, shoplifters can claim that they had fully intended to buy the shoplifted item, even if they've already stuffed it in a pocket or underneath their clothes.

that was there." The "I forgot" excuse, however, rarely gets anyone off the hook.

In most states, it is legal for store employees to detain a shoplifting suspect until the store determines how it wants to handle the matter. For the shoplifter, the best-case scenario is that security personnel decide to deal with the situation themselves without involving the police. Even then, they will definitely take back the stolen loot and most likely dole out a stern lecture, with a demand that the shoplifter never enter the store again. Security guards are also likely to make the confrontation with a shoplifter as public as possible to let the other customers know that they don't take shoplifting lightly.

For young offenders, one of their most dreaded fears is that security employees will tell their parents. In the *Newsweek* article "The Thrill of Theft," one teenage shoplifter explained her run-in with the mall police: "They arrested me and walked me through the mall; they took me to the juvenile center and called my parents. I got grounded for probably like a month and a half, but it was the first month of summer vacation, so it was really bad." The mall decided not to prose-cute the girl but demanded that she write a twenty-five-page paper about how shoplift-ing hurts retail stores and the economy.

In the Justice System

When stores decide to throw the book at shoplifters, their fate is still uncertain. The charges and punishments they face vary

In court, young shoplifters often get off with a warning or a fine. But even first-timers can find themselves subject to a harsher punishment if they appear before an unsympathetic judge.

Ten Great Questions to Ask Your Guidance Counselor

1 What is shoplifting?

2 Do teenagers shoplift more than adults?

3 Does anyone shoplift for a living?

4 What is employee theft?

5 Why would otherwise honest people shoplift?

6 What do stores do to prevent shoplifting?

7 How often do shoplifters get caught?

8 What punishments can shoplifters expect?

Who pays the price for shoplifting?

10 How can I help a friend or relative stop shoplifting?

five

HOW CAN SHOPLIFTERS GET HELP TO STOP?

For many shoplifters, getting caught is the best thing that could happen to them. It is a wake-up call that reminds them just how wrong shoplifting is and just how destructive it has become in their lives. An arrest forces shoplifters to confront their problem. When they do, most reach the same conclusion. Whatever gratification—either material or psychological—they get from shoplifting, it is just not worth the price.

But even with these realizations, not all shoplifters find it easy to quit. Some can decide not to shoplift, and that's that. Others, though, struggle to break what has become a very bad habit for them.

Shoplifting Education Programs

Shoplifters who want to change usually get little help from the criminal justice system. If they are sent to prison, they rarely receive any kind of treatment for their problem. Many people in the criminal justice system and in retail simply don't care about rehabilitating shoplifters. They share the sentiments of Richard Santoro, the former director of public affairs for the New Jersey Retail Merchants Association. In an article in the *Record*, a New Jersey newspaper, he explained, "We don't care why shoplifters shoplift. We care how they do it. What's [the stores'] incentive to care, really? People are surrounded by temptations every day. Either they know stealing's not the right thing to do or they're scared of the punishment—or not."

In private or group sessions, trained therapists can help teen shoplifters explore why they feel compelled to steal and discuss ways to stop their compulsive behavior.

However, in cases in which shoplifters do not receive prison time, judges may order them to enroll in a class to help discourage them from shoplifting again, usually stipulating that the shoplifters have to pay for the cost of the class themselves. Shoplifters might attend the class in person over several hours or take it over the Internet, whenever it is convenient for them. In these classes, students are asked to think about why they shoplift and reflect on the consequences of their crimes, both in terms of how shoplifting hurts society and how it has cost them personally. Critics of these programs hold that, although they might scare casual shoplifters straight, they do little to help compulsive shoplifters.

Sometimes, before going to court, people accused of shoplifting will take a class on their own. They hope that, by showing they are serious about not shoplifting again, they can persuade the judge to go easy on them.

Seeking Therapy

On their own, habitual shoplifters are sometimes hesitant to seek out help in dealing with their problem. They are too ashamed to tell their friends and relatives. They are also afraid to talk with a therapist or psychiatrist for fear of being turned over to the police. Mental health professionals, however, are not required to report shoplifters. Furthermore, they often have the knowledge and insight that can turn compulsive shoplifters into recovering shoplifters.

Therapists and counselors can identify underlying problems—such as depression or anxiety disorders—that drive many young people to act out by stealing.

When treating shoplifters addicted to the feelings of tension and relief that their stealing gives them, therapists try to figure out if their patients are suffering from an underlying psychological disorder. Depression is especially common among shoplifters. Getting patients to talk about their lives, therapists work to help them understand their feelings and determine other, better ways to relieve their negative emotions.

Psychiatrists, as medical doctors, might also give their patients prescription drugs, such as antidepressants, to help them cope better. Researchers are also experimenting with the use of a drug called naltexone to treat shoplifting. Already used to help alcoholics stop drinking, naltexone blocks certain nerve interactions in the brain, which lessens the rush that shoplifters get from stealing.

Many therapies and programs are designed to help shoplifters find "natural highs" that can replace the exhilaration of shoplifting. When they become overwhelmed by tension and anxiety, they are told to engage in some other activity that can soothe their nerves. Depending on the person, these activities might include calling a friend, reading a book, going to the movies, or exercising.

Rather than going into formal therapy, some shoplifters looking to stop attend support groups. In these groups, members discuss their problems with shoplifting and offer one another help and support in overcoming their compulsions. These support groups are similar to Alcoholics Anonymous (AA) meetings for people who have drinking problems. However, unlike AA meetings, which are widely available, there are very few support groups exclusively for shoplifters. Although it is now socially acceptable to admit to having problems with alcohol, many people still fear saying publicly that they have a problem with shoplifting. Increasingly, telephone and online support groups are available to encourage hesitant shoplifters to come forward and seek help.

Individual Strategies

Whether shoplifters work with therapists, attend support groups, or try to quit on their own, many come up with their own strategies to keep themselves from backsliding. For instance, they may try to avoid shopping in stores as much as possible. Instead, they choose to buy everything they need, including groceries, online. But not everyone needs such a radical approach. Instead, they might just avoid particular stores that seem to spark the urge to steal.

Many recovering shoplifters, before setting foot in a store, take a moment to assess their feelings. If they are angry, anxious, or depressed, they turn around and walk away. For many people, these emotions act as "triggers," encouraging them to shoplift to get relief from these painful feelings.

Other techniques involve a little advanced planning. Recovering shoplifters might still go to stores, but only in the company of non-shoplifting friends. Not wanting to shame themselves in front of their friends is a powerful reason to fight any shoplifting urge, no matter how intense.

Former shoplifters might also decide to shop only in retail outlets with good security systems—often the very places they

Going to stores with friends who don't steal can help teens struggling with a shoplifting habit to control their urges.

avoided in their shoplifting days. Just knowing there are plenty of security guards and cameras watching their every move can keep some recovering shoplifters honest. For a similar reason, they might strike up a conversation with a salesclerk or a security guard. By attracting attention to themselves, they are ensuring that employees will remember their faces, which makes it harder for recovering shoplifters to believe that they can steal and get away with it.

Many recovering shoplifters make a list of what they need to buy before going into a store. Focusing on the list, they gather everything they want quickly and get to the cashier before an urge to steal kicks in. Whenever they do feel the slightest urge, they immediately leave the store, whether they are done shopping or not.

Even just paying attention to what they are wearing can help some recovering shoplifters stay on the straight and narrow. They never go outside in big, roomy coats, under which they could hide merchandise. They also steer clear of any clothing with large pockets. Some women find it helpful to carry very small pocketbooks, with just enough room for their keys and wallets.

The strategies that compulsive shoplifters use to stop stealing differ. But all agree on one thing: becoming a recovering shoplifter is very hard work. Just like alcoholics and drug addicts, they can never see themselves as fully cured. Some days, they may feel fine and in control. But other days, the urge to shoplift will come over them again, seemingly out of nowhere. Then they have to summon all of their strength to resist it. If they don't, they run the risk of shoplifting again and facing all of the disasters that could come with it. They might be arrested and find themselves entangled in the legal system. They might lose the respect of those they care about most if their secret life is discovered. Moreover, they might endure needless pain and humiliation, overwhelmed by the feeling they have no control over their behavior.

One message should be clear: it is far easier never to shoplift than it is to stop shoplifting once it has become a compulsion. If you haven't shoplifted, count yourself lucky. If you have, the best thing you can do is to quit now before it's too late.

addiction The condition of being compelled to engage in a certain harmful activity.

booster A professional criminal who shoplifts for a living.

chain store One of a group of stores with the same owner that sells similar merchandise.

community service Unpaid work intended to help people in a community, often performed as a court-ordered alternative to a prison sentence.

compulsion An overwhelming urge.

consumer A person who purchases goods for his or her own use.

criminal record A list of the crimes a person has been convicted of.

depression A mental state often marked by sadness, inactivity, an inability to concentrate, and sometimes thoughts of suicide.

employee theft The stealing of goods from a store by someone who works there.

felony A major crime.

fence A criminal who resells stolen goods.

grand larceny A felony involving the theft of goods above a certain value determined by law.

habitual Done out of habit.

kleptomania A psychiatric condition that drives people to steal.

loss prevention industry Businesses designed to help stores limit shoplifting.

merchandise Goods offered for sale.

misdemeanor A minor crime.

petty larceny A misdemeanor involving the theft of goods under a certain value determined by law.

probation A sentence calling for an offender to check in regularly with an officer of the court in order to evaluate and monitor the offender's behavior.

retail The sale of goods to consumers for their own use.

sensor tag An anti-shoplifting device, attached to merchandise, that sets off an alarm when taken out of a store.

shoplift To take something from a retail store without paying for it.

shrink Lost income in retail stores due to stealing and administrative error.

surveillance Close observation, especially of a suspected criminal.

theft The act of committing the crime of stealing.

Loss Prevention Foundation

700 Matthews-Mint Hill Road, Suite C

Matthews, NC 28105

(704) 405-4404

Web site: http://www.losspreventionfoundation.org

The Loss Prevention Foundation is a nonprofit organization
that serves security professionals and experts who work
with retail stores to prevent shoplifting.

National Crime Prevention Council (NCPC)

2001 Jefferson Davis Highway, Suite 901

Arlington, VA 22202

(202) 466-6272

Web site: http://www.ncpc.org

NCPC educates people about what they can do to prevent
crime, including shoplifting.

Pathways Institute for Impulse Control

5758 Geary Boulevard, #227

San Francisco, CA 94121

(414) 267-6916

Web site: http://www.pathwaysinstitute.net

The Pathways Institute for Impulse Control is a treatment
center for people suffering from compulsive behaviors,
including habitual shoplifting.

Retail Council of Canada
1255 Bay Street, Suite 800
Toronto, ON M5R 2A9
Canada
(416) 922-6678
Web site: http://www.retailcouncil.org
The Retail Council of Canada promotes the interests of the
    retail industry and helps stores better serve their customers
    throughout Canada.

Shulman Center for Compulsive Theft and Spending
P.O. Box 250008
Franklin, MI 48025
(248) 358-8508
Web site: http://www.theshulmancenter.com
Operated by shoplifting expert Terrence Shulman, the
    Shulman Center is dedicated to helping people recover
    from a compulsion to shoplift and overspend.

Web Sites

Due to the changing nature of Internet links, Rosen Publishing
has developed an online list of Web sites related to the subject
of this book. This site is updated regularly. Please use this link to
access the list:

http://www.rosenlinks.com/faq/shop

Bailey, Jacqui. *Taking Action Against Youth Crime*. New York, NY: Rosen Publishing, 2009.

Ford, Jean Otto. *Rural Crime and Poverty*. Broomall, PA: Mason Crest Publishers, 2007.

Giddens, Sandra. *Obsessive-Compulsive Disorder* (Teen Mental Health). New York, NY: Rosen Publishing, 2009.

Juzwiak, Rich. *Addictive Personality* (Teen Mental Health). New York, NY: Rosen Publishing, 2009.

Krygier, Leora. *Juvenile Court: A Judge's Guide for Young Adults and Their Parents*. Lanham, MD: Scarecrow Press, 2009.

Levin, Judith. *Depression and Mood Disorders* (Teen Mental Health). New York, NY: Rosen Publishing, 2009.

Madison, Bennett. *The Blonde of the Joke*. New York, NY: HarperTeen, 2009.

Merino, Noel, ed. *Juvenile Crime*. Farmington Hills, MI: Greenhaven Press, 2010.

Pollack, Jenny. *Klepto*. New York, NY: Speak, 2008.

Toliver, Wendy. *Lifted*. New York, NY: Simon Pulse, 2010.

Tracy, Kristen. *Crimes of the Sarahs*. New York, NY: Simon Pulse, 2008.

Williams, Heidi. *Juvenile Crime*. Farmington Hills, MI: Greenhaven Press, 2010.

Index

A

alcohol abuse, 33, 52–53, 55
Alcoholics Anonymous (AA), 52
anorexia, 33
antidepressants, 52

B

booster bags, 15
boosters, 15
bulimia, 33, 35

C

Capriati, Jennifer, 35
chain stores, 17, 38
chemical imbalances, 31
closed-circuit television, 38
community service, 5, 44
compulsive shoplifters, 28–35,
    44, 50
computer chips, 28
criminal records, 44, 45
Cupchik, Will, 24

D

department stores, 4, 5, 7, 39
depression, 27, 30, 32, 52, 53
detectives, 38
discount stores, 16
drug abuse, 7, 15–16, 33, 55

E

eating disorders, 33, 35
education programs, 44, 48–50

emotional void, filling an,
    22–25
employee theft, 16–18, 46

F

false arrest, 40
felonies, 44
fences, 15–16, 38
flea markets, 16

G

gambling, 15, 31, 33, 35
gangs, 15, 38
gift cards, 18
Global Positioning System
    (GPS), 38
grand theft, 4, 44
guidance counselor, questions
    to ask your, 46–47

J

Josephson Institute of Ethics, 9
juvenile centers, 42

K

kleptomania, 28

L

lawsuits, 40
loss prevention industry, 11

M

misdemeanors, 44

About the Author

Liz Sonneborn is a writer living in Brooklyn, New York. A graduate of Swarthmore College, she is the author of numerous books for children, young adults, and adult readers. Sonneborn previously wrote *Frequently Asked Questions About Plagiarism*.

Photo Credits

Cover altrendo images/Altrendo/Getty Images; p. 6 Steve Grayson/WireImage/Getty Images; pp. 8–9 Image Source/Image Source/Getty Images; p. 11 Andre Kudyusov/Photodisc/Getty Images; p. 14 Joos Mind/Taxi/Getty Images; pp. 16–17 Greg Mathieson/Mai/Time & Life Images/Time & Life Pictures/Getty Images; pp. 20–21 © The Shulman Center for Compulsive Theft, Spending & Hoarding; p. 23 David Young-Wolff/Stone/Getty Images; pp. 30–31, 37, 41 Shutterstock; pp. 32–33 David Mack/Photo Researchers; p. 34 David Callow/AFP/Getty Images; pp. 42–43 © Bob Daemmrich/The Image Works; p. 49 © Mary Kate Denny/ PhotoEdit; p. 51 © Dennis MacDonald/PhotoEdit; p. 54 Brand X Pictures/Thinkstock.

Kathy Kuhtz Campbell; Photo Researcher: Marty Levick